First Facts®

PRO WRESTLING SUPERSTARS

WITHDRAWN

REY MYSTERIO

PRO WRESTLING SUPERSTAR

by Emily Raij

Consultant: Mike Johnson, writer
PWInsider.com

CAPSTONE PRESS
a capstone imprint

First Facts are published by Capstone Press,
1710 Roe Crest Drive, North Mankato, Minnesota 56003
www.capstonepub.com

Copyright © 2015 by Capstone Press, a Capstone imprint. All rights reserved. No part of this publication may be reproduced in whole or in part, or stored in a retrieval system, or transmitted in any form or by any means, electronic, mechanical, photocopying, recording, or otherwise, without written permission of the publisher.

Library of Congress Cataloging-in-Publication Data
Raij, Emily.
Rey Mysterio / by Emily Raij.
    pages cm. — (First facts. Pro wrestling superstars)
Includes bibliographical references and index.
Summary: "Profiles pro wrestler Rey Mysterio from his start in pro wrestling to possible future endeavors"— Provided by publisher.
ISBN 978-1-4914-2057-7 (library binding)
ISBN 978-1-4914-2263-2 (ebook PDF)
1. Rey Mysterio—Juvenile literature. 2. Wrestlers—United States—Juvenile literature. I. Title.

GV1196.M96R35 2015
796.812092—dc23
[B]
                                    2014023799

Editorial Credits
Nikki Bruno Clapper, editor; Aruna Rangarajan, designer;
Jo Miller, photo researcher; Katy LaVigne, production specialist

Photo Credits
Florida National Guard photo by Master Sgt. Thomas Kielbasa, 20; Getty Images: FilmMagic/Jill Ann Spaulding, 9, Frank Micelotta, 18, LatinContent/Jam Media/Alfredo Lopez, 10, 17; Michael Blair, 6; Newscom: SIPA/Revelli-Baeumont, 13, WENN Photos/Carrie Devorah, 14, WENN Photos/DM2, cover, ZUMA Press/Z Sports Images/Olivier Andrivon, 5

Design Elements
Shutterstock: i3alda, locote, optimarc

Printed in the United States of America in North Mankato, Minnesota.
092014   008482CGS15

TABLE OF CONTENTS

WWE Raw Tour, 2008

FACT

Rey has won every one of World Wrestling Entertainment's (WWE) five main championships. He has also won the Tag Team Championship.

BEATING THE ODDS

Rey Mysterio faced 28 wrestlers in the 2006 Royal Rumble. The last man standing would win. Rey fought hard to beat his final opponent, Randy Orton. But the match was postponed. Rey faced Orton again at WrestleMania. This time Rey had to fight a three-way **match** against Orton and Kurt Angle.

tag team—when two wrestlers partner together against other teams

match—a game or sporting competition

Rey (top) has competed against Randy Orton several times during his wrestling career.

In a three-way match, the first wrestler to **pin** another wins. Rey fought hard at WrestleMania and pinned Angle first. Rey was 5 feet, 6 inches (168 centimeters) tall and weighed 175 pounds (79 kilograms). At WrestleMania Rey became the lightest World Heavyweight Champion in WWE history. This small **luchador** had big dreams in the ring.

pin—to hold a wrestler firmly on his back for a certain length of time

luchador—a Spanish term for a professional wrestler in Mexico

BECOMING REY MYSTERIO

Rey Mysterio was born Oscar Gutiérrez on December 11, 1974. He was born in Chula Vista, California, near the Mexican border. On Friday nights he loved to watch his uncle Miguel wrestle in Mexico. Miguel wrestled in the traditional lucha libre style under the name Rey Misterio. Oscar wanted to become a professional wrestler just like his uncle. He began training at age 8.

FACT

Sometimes Oscar did as many as 500 push-ups in one workout.

Rey poses for the camera at a Las Vegas trade show in 2007.

Rey demonstrates his luchador skills against Jack Swagger.

LEARN ABOUT LUCHA LIBRE

Lucha libre is a Mexican style of high-flying pro wrestling. Most wrestlers wear masks. Smaller wrestlers often compete against bigger ones. Matches have heroes and villains. A hero is called a babyface in English and a *científico* or *técnico* in Spanish. A villain is a heel in English and a *rudo* in Spanish.

babyface—a wrestler who acts as a hero in the ring

heel—a wrestler who acts as a villain in the ring

Oscar first wrestled under the name Colibri, the Spanish word for "hummingbird." Wrestling **promoters** worried Oscar was too small and would get hurt. But Oscar got bigger and stronger. He gained fans all over Mexico. Before a match one day, Oscar's uncle Miguel gave him a new mask. Miguel proudly renamed him Rey Misterio Jr.

promoter—a person or company that puts on a sporting event

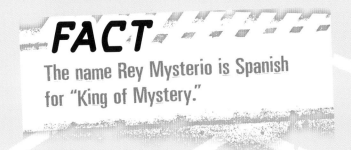

FACT
The name Rey Mysterio is Spanish for "King of Mystery."

RISING STAR

Rey's matches started being televised in Mexico. His nickname was Giant Killer. He proved he could beat larger wrestlers. Rey was fast, strong, and flexible. Fans quickly rallied around him. In 1995 he made the move to pro wrestling in the United States. Rey eventually joined the World Wrestling Federation (WWF). It is now called World Wrestling Entertainment (WWE).

Rey faced down many WWE "giants," such as Kane (left).

SIGNATURE MOVES

Rey has four popular wrestling moves. He does the West Coast Pop, the Frog Splash, the 619, and Droppin' Da Dime. Rey's acrobatic moves make for exciting matches.

Rey celebrating a win at WWE Cyber Sunday 2007

Rey shows his beliefs on his body. He has tattoos of religious symbols, his children's names, and his wife's picture. Skulls on his masks show the Mexican belief in life after death.

In lucha libre masks are important parts of a wrestler's image. Rey has about 500 masks.

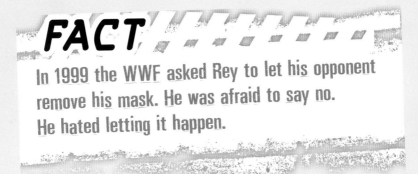

FACT

In 1999 the WWF asked Rey to let his opponent remove his mask. He was afraid to say no. He hated letting it happen.

Rey formed a wrestling **stable** called the Filthy Animals in 1999. He joined Konnan, Billy Kidman, and Eddie Guerrero. Later he teamed up with Sin Cara and others to win the Survivor Series. In this match groups fight to become the last team standing.

stable—a group of wrestlers who protect one another during matches and sometimes wrestle together

FACT

Rey and Guerrero trained together and were friends outside the ring. Sadly, Guerrero died of a heart attack in 2005. He was just 38 years old.

Rey greets his fans at
WWE SmackDown in 2007.

Slams from wrestlers such as Chris Jericho (right) have been tough on Rey.

Rey has had setbacks along with successes. Knee and arm injuries required surgeries and **rehabilitation**. Rey became **addicted** to painkillers. Then he got professional help to overcome his addiction. In 2012 Rey failed a WWE drug test. He denied drug use. The WWE punished him. He had to stop wrestling for two months.

rehabilitation—therapy that helps people recover their health or abilities

addicted—dependent on a drug or other substance

FAMILY AND SERVICE

Rey loves spending time with his wife, Angie, and their children. He also speaks to kids about standing up to bullying. Rey has been on three WWE Tribute to the Troops shows in Iraq. These shows entertain men and women in the U.S. military.

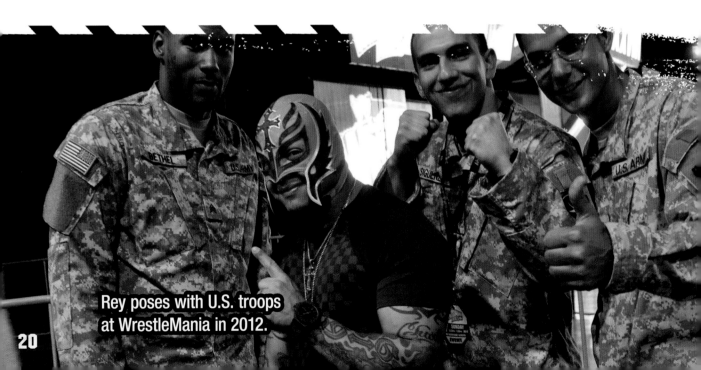

Rey poses with U.S. troops at WrestleMania in 2012.

TIMELINE

1974 – Rey is born on December 11.

1982 – Rey starts training in lucha libre.

1992 – Rey joins a Mexican wrestling league and wrestles under the name Colibri.

1995 – Rey joins Extreme Championship Wrestling under the name Rey Misterio Jr.

1996 – Rey marries Angie Gutiérrez.

1996 – Rey joins World Championship Wrestling (WCW).

1996 – Rey wrestles Dean Malenko to become WCW Cruiserweight Champion.

2002 – Rey joins WWE as Rey Mysterio.

2006 – Rey defeats Randy Orton and Kurt Angle to win the World Heavyweight Championship.

2008 – Rey, John Cena, and Batista beat another team of wrestlers at Tribute to the Troops.

GLOSSARY

addicted (uh-DIKT-ed)—dependent on a drug or other substance

babyface (BAY-bee-fayss)—a wrestler who acts as a hero in the ring

heel (HEEL)—a wrestler who acts as a villain in the ring

luchador (LOO-cha-dor)—a Spanish term for a professional wrestler in Mexico

match (MACH)—a game or sporting competition

pin (PIN)—to hold a wrestler firmly on his back for a certain length of time

promoter (pruh-MOH-tur)—a person or company that puts on a sporting event

rehabilitation (ree-huh-bil-uh-TAY-shun)—therapy that helps people recover their health or abilities

stable (STAY-buhl)—a group of wrestlers who protect one another during matches and sometimes wrestle together

tag team (TAG TEEM)—when two wrestlers partner together against other teams

READ MORE

Sullivan, Kevin. *Rey Mysterio.* DK Readers. New York: DK Pub., 2011.

Trejo, Aaron. *Rey Mysterio.* Torque: Pro Wrestling Champions. Minneapolis: Bellwether Media, 2012.

West, Tracey. *Rey Mysterio:* Giant Slayer. New York: Grosset & Dunlap, 2011.

INTERNET SITES

FactHound offers a safe, fun way to find Internet sites related to this book. All of the sites on FactHound have been researched by our staff.

Here's all you do:

Visit *www.facthound.com*

Type in this code: 9781491420577

Super-cool stuff!

Check out projects, games and lots more at
www.capstonekids.com

INDEX